The Modern Spirituality Series

# Dietrich Bonhoeffer

## *The Modern Spirituality Series*

Thomas Merton

Bede Griffiths

Dorothy Day

Dietrich Bonhoeffer

Henri Nouwen

Michael Ramsey

Rabbi Lionel Blue

John Main

Jean Vanier

Carlo Carretto

Metropolitan Anthony Bloom

**Dietrich Bonhoeffer in Tegel prison**

# Dietrich Bonhoeffer

Selections from his writings
Edited by Aileen Taylor
with an introduction by
Edwin Robertson

Templegate Publishers
Springfield, Illinois

First published in 1990 by
Darton, Longman and Todd Ltd
89 Lillie Road, London SW6 1UD

First published in 1992 in the United States by
Templegate Publishers
302 East Adams St./P.O. Box 5152
Springfield, IL 62705

ISBN 0-87243-198-3

# Contents

Introduction by Edwin Robertson                     11
Daily Readings with Dietrich Bonhoeffer             25
Sources and index                                   95

# Introduction

Dietrich Bonhoeffer was only thirty-nine when, near the end of a vicious war, he was taken out of his prison at Flossenburg and hanged as a traitor. 'Prisoner Bonhoeffer, come with me,' his jailer said, and he knew. The Lutheran pastor, who had resisted the injustices and persecutions of the National Socialists in Germany, had already lived many lives, although he still had much more to give. He left his cell saying to a companion, 'This is the end — but for me, the beginning of life.' At that fatal moment he could remember one person, and one event which had taken place less than three years before — in Sweden. There he had presented George Bell, the Bishop of Chichester, with peace plans that could have brought the war to an end in 1942. The mission failed; but as he was led out to die, Dietrich Bonhoeffer remembered his beloved bishop with the deep affection he had expressed in a letter, dated 1 June 1942, before he returned to Nazi Germany and the expectation of death:

> It will seem to me like a dream to have seen you, to have spoken to you, to have heard your voice. I think these days will remain in my memory as some of the greatest of my life. This spirit of fellowship and of Christian brotherliness will carry me through the darkest hour, and even if things go worse than we hope and expect, the light of these few days will never be extinguished in my heart.

Before 1942, Dietrich Bonhoeffer had lived a life of perception, courage and faithfulness, which made him an envoy whom those who risked their lives to overthrow Hitler and his government could trust with so dangerous a mission. Between 1942 and his execution on 9 April 1945, in freedom and in prison he faced the dilemmas of his Church struggling to avoid the consequences of a new world. Intellectually, he never flinched before a question, however devastating must be its answer.

*The cost of discipleship*

Dietrich Bonhoeffer was born on 4 February 1906 in Breslau. His family was comfortable, his father a successful psychotherapist, moving to Berlin when Dietrich was only six. There he was brought up, in an upper middle-class milieu which could never have been pleasanter than in the years before the First World War. He was a child during that war which radically changed his world: a brother killed, another wounded, the privations of the Allied blockade, the humility of defeat. A German through and through, he never forgave the Allies for the injustice of the Versailles Treaty.

Bonhoeffer's education was of the best and, to the surprise of his family, he opted for theology and the Church. It was a good time to be at university. After the post-war years of privation, he lived a fairly comfortable life and was a successful student at the universities of Tübingen and Berlin. A year in New York at Union Theological Seminary gave him a wider vision and a taste for the ecumenical movement, while his earlier assistant pastorate in Barcelona provided experience of pastoral work and preaching. He acquired a liking for Spanish culture and travelled in Mexico, Cuba, and Spain itself. He scarcely noticed the growing Nazi Party, but when he did, he acted at once. Within two days of Hitler's rise to power, he was broadcasting an attack on the exaltation of the leader in youth work. No one missed the fact that 'leader' was the same word in German as 'Führer' and his broadcast was cut short. He later circulated the entire manuscript. From then on, he saw National Socialism as the enemy. He was the first of the German theologians to speak out clearly against the persecution of the Jews.

When Adolf Hitler came to power on 30 January 1933, Dietrich Bonhoeffer was almost twenty-seven. He was already an established theologian with two important books of theology to his credit, and he was an experienced pastor and a lecturer. A good career was possible either as the minister of an influential church in Berlin or in an academic post at the university. But preferment at that time meant accepting the Führer as the savior of Germany and subscribing to the perverted theology of the so-called German Christians. He could do neither. He allied himself at once with the suffering Jews, and particularly with those of Jewish origin who, as Christians, sought to exercise a Christian ministry in the Church. He opposed the discrimination against the Jews and called for their just treatment as worthy German citizens. This

bold stand was dangerous and only the high connections of his family kept the Gestapo from
eliminating him. He joined with Martin Niemöller
in a resistance movement which led evenutally to
his death and Niemöller's long imprisonment.
Dietrich Bonhoeffer learnt early on 'the cost of
discipleship,' which was to become the title of his
most influential book. In it he showed how the Sermon on the Mount was no idealistic dream, but was
be lived in the everyday life of a Christian. The
book was not published until 1937, but he had
already started to live it.

Bonhoeffer wrote bravely about 'the Jewish
problem,' and from 1933 he was a marked man.
But he was young still, and unsure. He needed his
wilderness period to think through the consequences of his own convictions. In October 1933 he
found the opportunity in an invitation to serve two
German-speaking congregations in London.
Although Karl Barth strongly disapproved and told
him to come back, it was the first of a few vital
decisions which were turning-points in his life. In
London, he met George Bell, Bishop of
Chichester, whom he had already seen at an
ecumenical conference, and a close father-son relationship grew up between them. He provided Bell
with information about the church struggle in Germany and Bell provided him with spiritual
guidance. For two years, Bonhoeffer served the
congregations in London and in that time he grew
in stature.

Already, in Berlin, he had shown his ability to
care. When he was teaching a confirmation class of

boys from the poorer quarter of the city, he rented a flat in their area and opened it to any of them to use or simply to come and talk with him. In Barcelona, he had endeared himself to German exiles, visiting their homes. Here in London he found other expatriates and also an increasing number of refugees from Hitler's Germany. He ministered to these Germans and rallied other German-speaking congregations in England to support the Confessing Church, which from 1934 onwards became the main resistance in Germany to the sycophantic German Christians.

Bonhoeffer used his wilderness period well, broadening out from his Lutheran basis to encompass the spirituality of an ecumenical Church. Bell was his mentor. Much earlier, when Bonhoeffer and his brother had paid a visit to Rome, during Holy Week, Dietrich found a sympathetic Catholic priest who guided him through the liturgy of Holy Week in St Peter's and other churches. He was overwhelmed. He could argue theologically with his friend and remain firmly a Lutheran, but the Catholic liturgy and its spirituality conquered his heart. When later in his conspiratorial days he had to spend some time in the Benedictine monastery at Ettal, he confessed to being happy. Between the student visit to Rome and the more mature acceptance of monastic worship in Ettal lay a period of growth. He longed to visit Gandhi in India to learn of meditation, and Bishop Bell even arranged for him to stay at Gandhi's ashram. It was not to be. He was recalled to Germany, but not before he had experienced and seriously studied Anglican spirituality. He and a friend made short visits to Kelham, Mirfield and the Cowley Fathers at Oxford. The experience of those monastic ways of life greatly influenced his next task in Germany.

Bonhoeffer was recalled to establish a training center for ministerial students to serve the Confessing Church, which set itself up as an alternative to the German Christian state church. His seminary founded in the primitive conditions of a camp at Zingst on the Baltic Sea, was later transferred to a slightly more appropriate accommodation at Finkenwalde, near Stettin. Run on a shoe-string, it was one of the most unusual seminaries in Germany. Some thought it rather Catholic when he introduced Confession and somewhat mystical when he introduced Meditation. The students almost went into revolt when they were expected to read a text of the Bible for an hour, without discussing it and simply letting it speak to them. They learnt how to listen to the Word of God. Of course, there was thorough theological teaching and at the heart of the seminary was a community of brethren. Bonhoeffer incorporated much of what he had learnt in England from the Anglican monastic settlements. His devotion to Psalm 119 stands out. Most of his students recall particularly how he taught them to preach, pray and even listen to sermons. Those who came to Finkenwalde formed a close-knit community for the rest of their lives. It was there that Bonhoeffer completed his book *The Cost of Discipleship* and it was from the experiences in Finkenwalde that he wrote *Life Together*. The seminary ran for about two years and was then closed by the Gestapo in 1937. Bonhoeffer continued work with his students in clandestine group pastorates throughout Pomerania. His letters and theological papers continued to circulate until well into the war. He held together a network of well-trained pastors who would serve the churches well once the yoke of the Nazis had been broken.

In 1939, Germany was mobilized for war and Dietrich Bonhoeffer was eligible for military service. When placards appeared to say that those born in 1906 or 1907 were to register, it was not a call-up, but it presented Bonhoeffer with an immediate dilemma. The Confessing Church was not pacifist and Bonhoeffer did not want to harm his colleagues by a refusal to register. His greatest problem was that registration involved swearing an oath, not only of loyalty to Germany, which caused him no problem, but also to the Führer, which he could not do. He visited George Bell in Chichester for advice. The outcome was an invitation to lecture in America. He decided to go but he regarded it as a visit, while his friends looked upon it as a rescue plan and had ideas of his staying there for the duration of the war. They saw how valuable he would be in America; he saw how useless he would be after the war if he had spent the time in security. Much to his friends' disappointment, he left and returned to Germany within a few days. To one of the most influential of those friends, Reinhold Niebuhr, he wrote:

I have made a mistake in coming to America. I must live through this difficult period of our national history with the Christian people of Germany. I will have no right to participate in the reconstruction of Christian life in Germany after the war if I do not share the trials of this time with my people.

He saw that Christians in Germany faced a terrible alternative — either to will the defeat of their country in order to preserve civilization, or to will the victory of their country, which would mean the end of civilization. He knew which of these alternatives he would choose, but he could not take that decision in the security of America. So he returned to Germany, just before the outbreak of war. He knew the risks, and the limitations to be put upon his activities. He was forbidden to preach, to teach, to publish and even to convene groups for discussion. But he could still correspond with his students and meet them in secret.

He was not long back in Germany before his brother-in-law, Hans von Dohnanyi, persuaded him to join a conspiracy to overthrow Hitler. It was of long standing and active as early as the Munich Conference of 1938; but a state of war changes the nature of conspiracy. However, it continued in the Military Intelligence (the *Abwehr)* which was not accessible to the Gestapo. Bonhoeffer was enlisted for Military Intelligence because of his international contacts, but the purpose was to relieve him of any danger of conscription and to use him for the conspiracy. In this capacity, he travelled to

Switzerland and Sweden, both neutral countries, and kept in touch with leading figures of the ecumenical movement, including Visser 't Hooft and George Bell. The conspiracy had, by 1942, gathered an impressive support of military and political leaders. Bonhoeffer heard that Bell was going to Sweden and arranged to meet him there with the proposals of the conspiracy. These included the arrest of Hitler and a request that Great Britain would be prepared to treat with a non-Nazi government of Germany on honourable terms. Bell took the plans to Anthony Eden, but Winston Churchill turned them down, insisting on 'unconditional surrender.' Without that assurance, the military support fell away. The conspiracy continued with indifferent success until the attempt on Hitler's life on 20 July 1944, which resulted in the massacre of the élite of German leadership. But, by then, Bonhoeffer had been in prison for more than a year.

*Letters and Papers from Prison*

The events of his life had persuaded Dietrich Bonhoeffer that there was a need in those dark days to reconstruct Christian ethics. Before he was arrested on 5 April 1943 with others of his family, Bonhoeffer had started work on the subject. Scholars have struggled much with that unfinished book and it has been published in one form or another in most European languages. In English, it is called simply *Ethics*. It was his view that the dark, demonic dimensions of evil in his day demanded a total reconsideration of ethics. He helps us to face the modern world better equipped with ethical attitudes than our fathers were. Bonhoeffer continued to think about this book during his two years of prison life and wrote down many of his thoughts in letters, poems, sermons, plays and even a novel. He sent these to his friend and assistant at Finkenwalde, Eberhard Bethge, who has devoted his life to preserving and interpreting these writings.

The first book to appear, *Letters and Papers from Prison,* has become a spiritual classic. It depicts a man of great integrity and intelligence, wrestling with the problems of a failed Church in a world of darkness and sin. But it also shows Bonhoeffer's acceptance of secularism as a necessary stage of human development and his attempts to fashion a theology which accepts man's maturity as no longer in tutelage to God or the Church. The poems show his wrestling; the letters contain his longed-for discussions of the great religious themes and their relevance or irrelevance in the modern world. He tried to think of God in a secular way. His sermon for the baptism of Eberhard's first child shows his vision of the future, when the traditional words will be spoken again so that the world may believe. When Bethge gathered together all Bonhoeffer's papers — unpublished sermons, letters and lectures — in several volumes of *Collected Writings,* the later *Letters and Papers* were put in the context of a very precious life, which has turned the direction of theology in European thinking and opened up a new vein of spirituality.

When Dietrich Bonhoeffer was first arrested, it was on a minor charge and he expected to be released. Even when he was linked with Hans von Dohnanyi in the conspiracy, he still thought there was a chance of evading conviction; but after the failure of the July Plot, hope dwindled and he came to accept that sooner or later he would be executed. At the end, he ministered to his fellow-prisoners and on his last Sunday — the Sunday after Easter 1945 — those who heard the sermon he preached, and who survived, will never forget his assurance. The prisoners asked him to conduct a service. They were a mixed group of Protestants and Catholics, but that hardly mattered any more. There was one difficulty: Vasiliev Kokorin, Molotov's nephew, who tried to teach Bonhoeffer Russian, was an atheist. For his sake, Bonhoeffer would not conduct the service. Their solidarity during imprisonment could not be violated by separation. Not until Kokorin asked him would Bonhoeffer agree. Kokorin did not become a Christian, but he was part of that service. The text was: 'And with his stripes we are healed', with 'Blessed be the God and Father of our Lord Jesus Christ! By his great mercy we have been born anew to a living hope through the resurrection of our Lord Jesus Christ from the dead' (Isaiah 53:5; 1 Peter 1:3).

As Bonhoeffer accepted death, he wondered often why he could not be preserved to help in the reconstruction of Christian life in Germany after the war. It was so near. He had returned from America for this, and he could now hear the bombardment as the Americans advanced. The war was

**21**

already lost and won. It seemed so pointless that he should die then. But this too he accepted, and he expressed his acceptance in his poem 'The Death of Moses.'

Upon the mountain's summit stands at last
Moses the prophet and the man of God.
Unwavering his eyes look on the view,
survey the promised scene, the holy land.
'Now, Lord, thy promises have been fulfilled,
to me thy word has been for ever sure...
So now today, inflict my punishment,
enfold me in the long dark sleep of death.
Rich grow the vineyards in the holy land;
faith only knows the promise of their wine...
God, quick to punish sin or to forgive,
thou knowest how this people has my love.
Enough that I have borne its shame and sacrifice
and seen salvation—now I need not live.'

It is not difficult to see how this young man of thirty-nine, who longed to take part in the reconstruction of Christian life in his poisoned land, found identity with the aged Moses.

EDWIN ROBERTSON

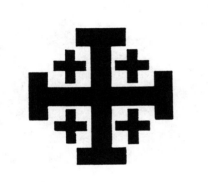

# Giving thanks

Only he who gives thanks for little things receives the big things. We prevent God from giving us the great spiritual gifts he has in store for us, because we do not give thanks for daily gifts.

We think we dare not be satisfied with the small measure of spiritual knowledge, experience, and love that has been given to us, and that we must constantly be looking forward eagerly for the highest good. Then we deplore the fact that we lack the deep certainty, the strong faith, and the rich experience that God has given to others, and we consider this lament to be pious.

We pray for the big things and forget to give thanks for the ordinary, small (and yet really not small) gifts. How can God entrust great things to one who will not thankfully receive from him the little things? If we do not give thanks daily for the Christian fellowship in which we have been placed, even where there is no great experience, no discoverable riches, but much weakness, small faith, and difficulty; then we hinder God from letting our fellowship grow according to the measure and riches which are there for us all in Jesus Christ.

## *Spiritual stillness*

Silence is the simple stillness of the individual under the Word of God. We are silent before hearing the word because our thoughts are already directed to the Word, as a child is quiet when he enters his father's room. We are silent after hearing the Word because the Word is still speaking and dwelling within us. We are silent at the beginning of the day because God should have the first word, and we are silent before going to sleep because the last word also belongs to God.

Silence is nothing else but waiting for God's Word and coming from God's Word with a blessing. But everybody knows that this is something that needs to be practiced and learned, in these days when talkativeness prevails. Real silence, real stillness, really holding one's tongue come only as the sober consequence of spiritual stillness.

But this stillness before the Word will exert its influence upon the whole day. If we have learned to be silent before the Word, we shall also learn to manage our silence and our speech during the day.

The silence of the Christian is listening silence, humble stillness, that may be interrupted at any time for the sake of humility.

## *Freedom in the fellowship*

A Christian community should know that somewhere in it there will certainly be 'a reasoning among them, which of them should be the greatest.' It is the struggle of the natural man for self-justification. He finds it only in comparing himself with others, in condemning and judging others. Self-justification and judging others go together, as justification by grace and serving others go together.

It must be a decisive rule of every Christian fellowship that each individual is prohibited from saying much that occurs to him.

Where this discipline of the tongue is practiced right from the beginning, each individual will make a matchless discovery. He will be able to cease from constantly scrutinizing the other person, judging him, condemning him, putting him in his particular place where he can gain ascendancy over him and thus doing violence to him as a person.

Now he can allow the brother to exist as a completely free person, as God made him to be. Now the other person, in the freedom with which he was created, becomes the occasion of joy, whereas before he was only a nuisance and an affliction.

# The ministry of listening

The first service that one owes to others in the fellowship consists in listening to them. Just as love to God begins with listening to his Word, so the beginning of love for the brethren is learning to listen to them. It is God's love for us that he not only gives us his Word but also lends us his ear. So it is his work that we do for our brother when we learn to listen to him.

Christians, especially ministers, so often think they must always contribute something when they are in the company of others, that this is the one service they have to render. They forget that listening can be a greater service than speaking.

He who can no longer listen to his brother will soon be no longer listening to God either; he will be doing nothing but prattle in the presence of God too. This is the beginning of the death of the spiritual life, and in the end there is nothing left but spiritual chatter and clerical condescension arrayed in pious words.

Christians have forgotten that the ministry of listening has been committed to them by him who is himself the great listener and whose work they should share.

# The ministry of bearing

The law of Christ is a law of bearing. Bearing means forbearing and sustaining.

The Christian must bear the burden of a brother. He must suffer and endure the brother.

God took men upon himself and they weighted him to the ground. In bearing with men God maintained fellowship with them. It is the law of Christ that was fulfilled in the cross. And Christians must share in this law.

It is, first of all, the freedom of the other person, of which we spoke earlier, that is a burden to the Christian. The other's freedom collides with his own autonomy, yet he must recognize it. He could get rid of this burden by refusing the other person his freedom, by constraining him and thus doing violence to his personality, by stamping his own image upon him. But if he lets God create his image in him, he by this token gives him his freedom and himself bears the burden of this freedom of another creature of God.

The freedom of the other person includes all that we mean by a person's nature, individuality, endowment. It also includes his weaknesses and oddities, which are such a trial to our patience, everything that produces frictions, conflicts, and collisions among us.

# The ministry of proclaiming

Where Christians live together the time must inevitably come when in some crisis one person will have to declare God's word and will to another.

It is inconceivable that the things that are of utmost importance to each individual should not be spoken by one to another. It is unchristian consciously to deprive another of the one decisive service we can render to him. If we cannot bring ourselves to utter it, we shall have to ask ourselves whether we are not still seeing our brother garbed in his human dignity which we are afraid to touch, and thus forgetting the most important thing, that he, too, no matter how old or highly placed or distinguished he may be, is still a man like us, a sinner in crying need of God's grace.

He has the same great necessities that we have, and needs help, encouragement, and forgiveness as we do. The basis upon which Christians can speak to one another is that each knows the other as a sinner, who, with all his human dignity, is lonely and lost if he is not given help.

This recognition gives to our brotherly speech the freedom and candor that it needs.

# Message of liberation

It may be that Christians, notwithstanding corporate worship, common prayer and all their fellowship in service, may still be left to their loneliness.

The final breakthrough to fellowship does not occur, because, though they have fellowship with one another as believers and as devout people, they do not have fellowship as the undevout, as sinners.

The pious fellowship permits no one to be a sinner. So everybody must conceal his sin from himself and from the fellowship. We dare not be sinners.

Many Christians are unthinkably horrified when a real sinner is suddenly discovered among the righteous. So we remain alone with our sin, living in lies and hypocrisy. The fact is that we *are* sinners!

But it is the grace of the gospel, which is so hard for the pious to understand, that it confronts us with the truth and says: You are a sinner, a great, desperate sinner; now come, as the sinner that you are, to God who loves you. He wants you as you are; he does not want anything from you, a sacrifice, a work; he wants you alone. 'My son, give me thine heart' (Proverbs 23:26). God has come to you to save the sinner. Be glad!

# Confession

It was none other than Jesus Christ himself who suffered the scandalous, public death of a sinner in our stead. He was not ashamed to be crucified for us as an evildoer. It is nothing else but our fellowship with Jesus Christ that leads us to the ignominious dying that comes in confession, in order that we may in truth share in his cross.

The cross of Jesus Christ destroys all pride. We cannot find the cross of Jesus if we shrink from going to the place where it is to be found, namely, the public death of the sinner. And we refuse to bear the cross when we are shamed to take upon ourselves the shameful death of the sinner in confession.

In confession we break through to the true fellowship of the cross of Jesus Christ, in confession we affirm and accept our cross. In the deep mental and physical pain of humiliation before a brother — which means, before God — we experience the cross of Jesus as our rescue and salvation. The old man dies, but it is God who has conquered him.

Now we share in the resurrection of Christ and eternal life.

# The call to discipleship

To follow in his steps is something which is void of all content, it gives us no intelligible programme for a way of life, no goal or ideal to strive after. It is not a cause which human calculation might deem worthy of our devotion.

What happens? At the call, Levi leaves all that he has — but not because he thinks that he might be doing something worth while, but simply for the sake of the call. The disciple simply burns his boats and goes ahead. He is called out, and has to forsake his old life in order that he may 'exist' in the strictest sense of the word.

It is nothing else than bondage to Jesus Christ alone, completely breaking through every programme, every ideal, every set of laws. No other significance is possible, since Jesus is the only significance. Apart from Jesus nothing has any significance. He alone matters.

When we are called to follow Christ, we are summoned to an exclusive attachment to his person. The grace of his call bursts all the bonds of legalism. It is a gracious call, a gracious commandment.

Christ calls, the disciple follows; that is grace and commandment in one.

# A definite step

The call to follow implies that there is only one way of believing in Jesus Christ, and that is by leaving all and going with the incarnate Son of God.

The first step places the disciple in the situation where faith is possible. If he refuses to follow and stays behind, he does not learn how to believe.

So long as Levi sits at the receipt of custom, and Peter at his nets, they could both pursue their trade honestly and dutifully, and they might both enjoy religious experiences, old and new. But if they want to believe in God, the only way is to follow his incarnate Son.

Until that day, everything had been different. They could remain in obscurity, pursuing their work as the quiet in the land, observing the law and waiting for the coming of the Messiah. But now he has come, and his call goes forth. Faith can no longer mean sitting still and waiting — they must rise and follow him. The call frees them from all earthly ties, and binds them to Jesus Christ alone.

The road to faith passes through obedience to the call of Jesus. Unless a definite step is demanded, the call vanishes into thin air.

# The cross

'If any man would come after me, let him deny himself.' The disciple must say to himself the same words Peter said of Christ when he denied him: 'I know not this man.' To deny oneself is to be aware only of Christ and no more of self, to see only him who goes before and no more the road which is too hard for us.

If in the end we know only him, if we have ceased to notice the pain of our own cross, we are indeed looking only unto him.

To endure the cross is not a tragedy; it is the suffering which is the fruit of an exclusive allegiance to Jesus Christ. It is not the sort of suffering which is inseparable from this mortal life, but the suffering which is an essential part of the specifically Christian life.

If our Christianity has ceased to be serious about discipleship, if we have watered down the gospel into emotional uplift which makes no costly demands and which fails to distinguish between natural and Christian existence, then we cannot help regarding the cross as an ordinary everyday calamity, as one of the trials and tribulations of life.

## *His yoke is easy*

For God is a God who *bears*. The Son of God bore
our flesh, he bore the cross, he bore our sins, thus
making atonement for us.

In the same way his followers are also called upon
to bear, and that is precisely what it means to be a
Christian. Just as Christ maintained his communion with the Father by his endurance, so his
followers are to maintain their communion with
Christ by their endurance.

Jesus invites all who travail and are heavy laden to
throw off their own yoke and take his yoke upon
them — and his yoke is easy, and his burden is light.
The yoke and the burden of Christ are his cross.

To go one's way under the sign of the cross is not
misery and desperation, but peace and refreshment
for the soul, it is the highest joy. Then we do not
walk under our self-made laws and burdens, but
under the yoke of him who knows us and who
walks under the yoke with us. Under his yoke we
are certain of his nearness and communion. It is he
whom the disciple finds as he lifts up his cross.

# *The individual*

Through the call of Jesus men become individuals. Every man is called separately, and must follow alone.

The call of Jesus teaches us that our relation to the world has been built on an illusion. All the time we thought we had enjoyed a direct relation with men and things. Now we learn that in the most intimate relationships of life, in our kinship with father and mother, brothers and sisters, in married love, and in our duty to the community, direct relationships are impossible.

We are separated from one another by an unbridgeable gulf of otherness and strangeness which resists all our attempts to overcome it by means of natural association or emotion or spiritual union. There is no way from one person to another.

However loving and sympathetic we may try to be, however sound our psychology, however frank and open our behavior, we cannot penetrate the incognito of the other man, for there are no direct relationships, not even between soul and soul. Christ stands between us, and we can only get in touch with our neighbors through him.

This is certain: in one way or the other we shall have to leave the immediacy of the world and become individuals.

# Overcome evil with good

'Blessed are the peacemakers: for they shall be called the children of God.' The followers of Jesus have been called to peace. When he called them they found their peace, for he is their peace.

But now they are told that they must not only *have* peace but *make* it. And to that end they renounce all violence and tumult. In the cause of Christ nothing is to be gained by such methods. His kingdom is one of peace, and the mutual greeting of his flock is a greeting of peace.

His disciples keep the peace by choosing to endure suffering themselves rather than inflict it on others. They maintain fellowship where others would break it off. They renounce all self-assertion, and quietly suffer in the face of hatred and wrong. In so doing they overcome evil with good, and establish the peace of God in the midst of a world of war and hate.

But nowhere will that peace be more manifest than where they meet the wicked in peace and are ready to suffer at their hands.

Now that they are partners in Christ's work of reconciliation, they are called the sons of God as he is the Son of God.

# The law is fulfilled

Jesus Christ — and he alone — fulfills the law, because he alone lives in perfect communion with God.

It is Jesus himself who comes between the disciples and the law, not the law which comes between Jesus and the disciples.

They are faced not with a law which has never yet been fulfilled, but with one whose demands have already been satisfied. The righteousness it demands is already there, the righteousness of Jesus which submits to the cross because that is what the law demands. This righteousness is therefore not a duty owed, but a perfect and truly personal communion with God, and Jesus not only possesses this righteousness, but is himself the personal embodiment of it.

He is the righteousness of the disciples. By calling them he had admitted them to partnership with himself, and made them partakers of his righteousness in its fullness.

Of course the righteousness of the disciples can never be a personal achievement; it is always a gift, which they received when they were called to follow him. In fact their righteousness consists precisely in their following him, and in the beatitudes the reward of the kingdom of heaven has been promised to it.

# Pacifism

When a Christian meets with injustice, he no longer clings to his rights and defends them at all costs. He is absolutely free from possessions and bound to Christ alone.

The only way to overcome evil is to let it run itself to a standstill because it does not find the resistance it is looking for. When evil meets no opposition and encounters no obstacle but only patient endurance, its sting is drawn. By his willingly renouncing self-defence, the Christian affirms his absolute adherence to Jesus, and his freedom from the tyranny of his own ego.

He addresses his disciples as men who have left all to follow him, and the precept of non-violence applies equally to private life and official duty.

It looked as though evil had triumphed on the cross, but the real victory belonged to Jesus. Jesus calls those who follow him to share his passion. How can we convince the world by our preaching of the passion when we shrink from that passion in our own lives? The cross is the only power in the world which proves that suffering love can avenge and vanquish evil.

# The Sermon on the Mount

The better righteousness of the disciples must have a motive which lies beyond itself.

We are confronted with a paradox. Our activity must be visible, but never be done for the sake of making it visible. 'Let your light so shine before men' (Matthew 5:16) and yet: Take care that you hide it ! There is a pointed contrast between [Matthew] chapters 5 and 6. That which is visible must also be hidden.

From whom are we to hide the visibility of our discipleship? Certainly not from other men, for we are told to let them see our light. No. We are to hide it from *ourselves*. Our task is simply to keep on following, looking only to our Leader who goes on before, taking no notice of ourselves or of what we are doing. We must be unaware of our own righteousness.

If the left hand knows what the right hand is doing, if we become conscious of our hidden virtue, we are forging our own reward, instead of that which God had intended to give us in his own good time. But if we are content to carry on with our life hidden from our eyes, we shall receive our reward openly from God.

# *Prayer*

We pray to God because we believe in him through Jesus Christ; that is to say, our prayer can never be an entreaty to God, for we have no need to come before him in that way. We are privileged to know that he knows our needs before we ask him.

Genuine prayer is never 'good works,' an exercise or a pious attitude, but it is always the prayer of a child to a Father. Hence it is never given to self-display, whether before God, ourselves, or other people. If God were ignorant of our needs we should have to think out beforehand *how* we should tell him about them, *what* we should tell him, and whether we should tell him or not.

Thus faith, which is the mainspring of Christian prayer, excludes all reflection and premeditation. How are we to be protected from ourselves, and our own premeditations?

The only way is by mortifying our own wills which are always obtruding themselves. And the only way to do this is by letting Christ alone reign in our hearts, by surrendering our wills completely to him, by living in fellowship with Jesus and by following him. Then we can pray that his will may be done, the will of him who knows our needs before we ask.

# The Lord's Prayer

Jesus told his disciples not only *how* to pray, but also *what* to pray. The Lord's Prayer is not merely the pattern prayer; it is the way Christians *must* pray. If they pray this prayer, God will certainly hear them.

The call of Jesus binds them into a brotherhood. In the name of the son of God they are privileged to call God Father.

God's name, God's kingdom, God's will must be the primary object of Christian prayer. Of course it is not as if God needed our prayers, but they are the means by which the disciples become partakers in the heavenly treasure for which they pray.

'Give us this day our daily bread.' As long as the disciples are on earth, they should not be ashamed to pray for their bodily needs.

'Forgive us our debts, as we also forgive our debtors. Every day Christ's followers    must acknowledge and bewail their guilt.

'Lead us not into temptation.' Christians ask God not to put their puny faith to the test, but to preserve them in the hour of temptation.

'But deliver us from evil.' The last petition is for deliverance from evil and for the inheritance of the kingdom of heaven.

# The carefree life

What are we really devoted to? That is the question. Are our hearts set on earthly goods? Do we try to combine devotion to them with loyalty to Christ? Or are we devoted exclusively to him?

The light of the body is the eye, and the light of the Christian is his heart. If the eye be dark, how great is the darkness of the body! But the heart is dark when it clings to earthly goods, for then, however urgently Jesus may call us, his call fails to find access to our hearts. Our hearts are closed, for they have already been given to another.

As the light cannot penetrate the body when the eye is evil, so the word of Jesus cannot penetrate the disciple's heart so long as it is closed against it. The word is choked like the seed which was sown among thorns, choked 'with cares and riches and pleasures of this life' (Luke 8:14).

Jesus does not forbid the possession of property in itself. He was man, he ate and drank like his disciples, and thereby sanctified the good things of life. Earthly goods are given to be used, not to be collected.

Hoarding is idolatry.

## The narrow path

To be called to a life of extraordinary quality, to live up to it, and yet to be unconscious of it is indeed a narrow way. To confess and testify to the truth as it is in Jesus, and at the same time to love the enemies of that truth, his enemies and ours, and to love them with the infinite love of Jesus Christ, is indeed a narrow way.

To believe the promise of Jesus that his followers shall possess the earth, and at the same time to face our enemies unarmed and defenceless, preferring to incur injustice rather than do wrong ourselves, is indeed a narrow way. To see the weakness and wrong in others, and at the same time refrain from judging them; to deliver the gospel message without casting pearls before swine, is indeed a narrow way.

If we behold Jesus Christ going on before, step by step, we shall not go astray. But if we worry about the dangers that beset us, if we gaze at the road instead of at him who goes before, we are already straying from the path. For he is himself the way, the narrow way and the strait gate. He, and he alone, is our journey's end.

# *A home*

Most people have forgotten nowadays what a home can mean, though some of us have come to realize it as never before. It is a kingdom of its own in the midst of the world, a stronghold amid life's storms and stresses, a refuge, even a sanctuary.

It is not founded on the shifting sands of outward or public life, but it has its peace in God, for it is God who gives it its special meaning and value, and its own nature and privilege, its own destiny and dignity.

It is an ordinance of God in the world, the place in which — whatever may happen in the world — peace, quietness, joy, love, purity, discipline, respect, obedience, tradition, and, with it all, happiness may dwell. Not novelty, but permanence; not change, but constancy; not noisiness, but peace; not words, but deeds; not commands, but persuasion; not desire, but possession...

In a word, live together in the forgiveness of your sins, for without it no human fellowship can survive. Don't insist on your rights, don't blame each other, don't judge or condemn each other, don't find fault with each other, but accept each other as you are, and forgive each other every day from the bottom of your hearts.

# Composure? Indifference?

When things like this happen, I see that composure isn't part of my nature...I read in Lessing recently: 'I am too proud to consider myself unlucky. Just clench your teeth and let your skiff sail where the wind and waves take it. Enough that I do not intend to upset it myself.'

Is this pride and teeth-clenching to be completely forbidden and alien to the Christian, and replaced by a soft composure that gives way prematurely? Is there not also a kind of composure which proudly clenches its teeth, but is quite different from a dull, stolid, rigid, lifeless, mechanical submitting-to-something-I can't-help?

I think we honor God more if we gratefully accept the life that he gives us with all its blessings, loving it and drinking it to the full, and also grieving deeply and sincerely when we have impaired or wasted any of the good things of life...than if we are insensitive to life's blessings and may therefore also be insensitive to pain.

Job's words, 'The Lord gave...' include rather than exclude this, as can be seen clearly enough from his teeth-clenching speeches which were vindicated by God in the face of the false, premature, pious submission of his friends.

# Comforting

You may know that the last few nights have been bad...Those who had been bombed out came to me the next morning for a bit of comfort. But I'm afraid I'm bad at comforting; I can listen all right, but I can hardly find anything to say.

But perhaps the way one asks about some things and not about others helps to suggest what really matters; and it seems to me more important actually to share someone's distress than to use smooth words about it.

I've no sympathy with some wrong-headed attempts to explain away distress, because instead of being comfort, they are the exact opposite.

So I don't try to explain it, and I think that is the right way to begin, although it's only a beginning, and I very seldom get beyond it.

I sometimes think that real comfort must break in just as unexpectedly as the distress.

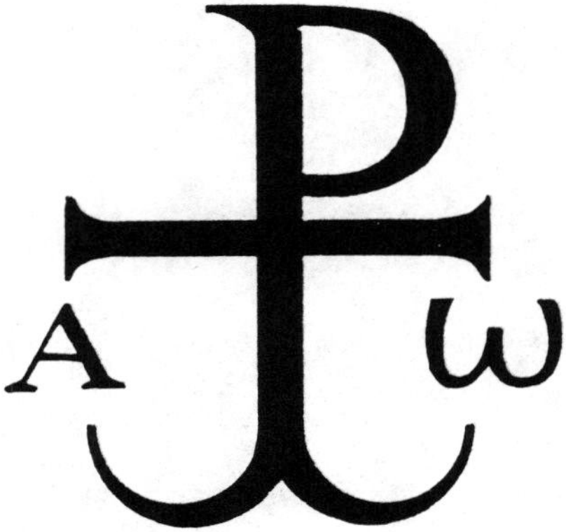
A
ω

# *Fate — guidance?*

I've often wondered here where we are to draw the line between necessary resistance to 'fate,' and equally necessary submission.

I think we must rise to the great demands that are made on us personally, and yet at the same time fulfill the commonplace and necessary tasks of daily life.

We must confront fate — to me the neuter gender of the word 'fate' (Schicksal) is significant — as resolutely as we submit to it at the right time. One can speak of 'guidance' only on the other side of that twofold process, with God meeting us no longer as 'Thou,' but also 'disguised' in the 'It'; so in the last resort my question is how we are to find the 'Thou' in this 'It' (that is, fate), or, in other words, how does 'fate' really become 'guidance'?

It's therefore impossible to define the boundary between resistance and submission on abstract principles; but both of them must exist, and both must be practiced.

Faith demands this elasticity of behavior. Only so can we stand our ground in each situation as it arises, and turn it to gain.

# *Suffering*

Perhaps we've made too much of this question of suffering, and been too solemn about it. I've sometimes been surprised that the Roman Catholics take so little notice of that kind of thing. Is it because they're stronger than we are? Perhaps they know better from their own history what suffering and martyrdom really are, and are silent about petty inconveniences and obstacles.

I believe, for instance, that physical sufferings, actual pain and so on, are certainly to be classed as 'suffering.' We so like to stress spiritual suffering; and yet that is just what Christ is supposed to have taken from us, and I can find nothing about it in the New Testament, or in the acts of the early martyrs.

After all, whether 'the Church suffers' is not at all the same as whether one of its servants has to put up with this or that.

I think we need a good deal of correction on this point; indeed, I must admit candidly that I sometimes feel almost ashamed of how often we've talked about our own suffering. No, suffering must be something quite different, and have a quite different dimension, from what I've so far experienced.

# A completely religionless time

What is bothering me incessantly is the question what Christianity really is, or indeed who Christ really is, for us today.

The time when people could be told everything by means of words, whether theological or pious, is over, and so is the time of inwardness and conscience — and that means the time of religion in general. We are moving towards a completely relgionless time; ...if our final judgment must be that the western form of Christianity was only a preliminary step to a complete absence of religion, what kind of situation emerges for us, for the Church?

What do a Church, a community, a sermon, a liturgy, a Christian life mean in a religionless world? How do we speak of God — without religion, that is, without the temporally conditioned presuppositions of metaphysics, inwardness, and so on?

How do we speak...in a 'secular' way about 'God'? In what way are we 'religionless-secular' Christians, in what way are we — those who are called forth — not regarding ourselves from a religious point of view as specially favoured, but rather as belonging wholly to the world?

In that case Christ is no longer an object of religion, but something quite different, really the Lord of the world.

# At the center

Religious people speak of God when human knowledge (perhaps simply because they are too lazy to think) has come to an end, or when human resources fail—in fact it is always the 'deus ex machina' that they bring on to the scene, either for the apparent solution of insoluble problems, or as strength in human failure—always, that is to say, exploiting human weakness or human boundaries.

I should like to speak of God not on the boundaries but at the center, not in weakness but in strength; and therefore not in death and guilt but in man's life and goodness. As to the boundaries, it seems to me better to be silent and leave the insoluble unsolved.

Belief in the resurrection is not the 'solution' of the problem of death. God's 'beyond' is not the beyond of our cognitive faculties. God is beyond in the midst of our life.

The Church stands, not at the boundaries where human powers give out, but in the middle of the village. That is how it is in the Old Testament, and in this sense we still read the New Testament far too little in the light of the Old.

# The new language

Our Church, which has been fighting in these years only for its self-preservation, as though that were an end in itself, is incapable of taking the word of reconciliation and redemption to mankind and the world.

Our earlier words are therefore bound to lose their force and cease, and our being Christians today will be limited to two things: prayer and righteous action among men. All Christian thinking, speaking, and organizing must be born anew out of this prayer and action.

We are not yet out of the melting-pot, and any attempt to help the Church prematurely to a new expansion of its organization will merely delay its conversion and purification.

It is not for us to prophesy the day (though the day will come) when men will once more be called so to utter the Word of God that the world will be changed and renewed by it. It will be a new language, perhaps quite non-religious, but liberating and redeeming — as was Jesus' language; it will shock people and yet overcome them by its power; it will be the language of a new righteousness and truth, proclaiming God's peace with men and the coming of his kingdom.

## To realize his presence

How wrong it is to use God as a stop-gap for the incompleteness of our knowledge. If in fact the frontiers of knowledge are being pushed further and further back (and that is bound to be the case), then God is being pushed back with them, and is therefore continually in retreat. We are to find God in what we know, not in what we don't know; God wants us to realize his presence, not in unsolved problems but in those that are solved.

It is simply not true to say that only Christianity has the answers to them. It may be that the Christian answers are just as unconvincing—or convincing—as any others.

Here again, God is no stop-gap; he must be recognized at the center of life, not when we are at the end of our resources; it is his will to be recognized in life, and not only when death comes; in health and vigor, and not only in suffering; in our activities, and not only in sin.

The ground for this lies in the revelation of God in Jesus Christ. He is the center of life, and he certainly didn't 'come' to answer our unsolved problems.

## God of weakness

God would have us know that we must live as men who manage our lives without him. The God who is with us is the God who forsakes us (Mark 15:34). The God who lets us live in the world without the working hypothesis of God is the God before whom we stand continually.

Before God and with God we live without God. God lets himself be pushed out of the world on to the cross. He is weak and powerless in the world, and that is precisely the way, the only way, in which he is with us and helps us.

Christ helps, not by virtue of his omnipotence, but by virtue of his weakness and suffering.

Here is the decisive difference between Christianity and all religions. Man's religiosity makes him look in his distress to the power of God in the world: God is the 'deus ex machina.' The Bible directs man to God's powerlessness and suffering; only the suffering God can help.

To that extent we may say that the development towards the world's coming of age, which had done away with a false conception of God, opens up a way of seeing the God of the Bible, who wins power and space in the world by his weakness.

## To be a Christian

To be a Christian does not mean to be religious in a particular way, to make something of oneself (a sinner, a penitent, or a saint) on the basis of some method or other, but to be a man — not a type of man, but the man that Christ creates in us.

It is not the religious act that makes the Christian, but participation in the sufferings of God in the secular life. That is 'metanoia': not in the first place thinking about one's own needs, problems, sins, and fears, but allowing onself to be caught up into the way of Jesus Christ, into the messianic event. Jesus calls men, not to a new religion, but to life.

But what does this life look like, this participation in the powerlessness of God in the world? When we speak of God in a 'non-religious' way, we must speak of him in such a way that the godlessness of the world is not in some way concealed, but rather revealed, and thus exposed to an unexpected light.

The world that has come of age is more godless, and perhaps for that very reason nearer to God, than the world before its coming of age.

## Each new day

Each new day is a new beginning in our life. Each day is a self-contained whole. Today is the limit of our cares and concerns. Today is long enough to find God or to lose him, to keep the faith or to succumb to sin and shame.

God created day and night so that we should not wander in boundless space but in the morning already see before us our evening's destination.

Just as the old sun is new each day it rises, so too the eternal mercy of God is new every morning. To understand God's old faithfulness anew every morning, to be able to begin a new life with God in the midst of a life with God, is the gift that God gives us every morning.

When we wake we can drive away the dark shades of night and the confusions of our dreams by immediately uttering the morning blessing and commending ourselves on this day to the help of the triune God.

Before the ear perceives the countless voices of the day it must listen in the early morning to the voice of the Creator and Redeemer. God has prepared the stillness of the earliest morning for himself. It must belong to him.

# Community

We belong to one another only through and in Jesus Christ...The Christian is the man who no longer seeks his salvation, his deliverance, his justification in himself, but in Jesus Christ alone. He knows that God's Word in Jesus Christ pronounces him guilty, even when he does not feel his guilt, and God's Word in Jesus Christ pronounces him not guilty and righteous, even when he does not feel that he is righteous at all.

Our righteousness is an 'alien righteousness,' a righteousness that comes from outside of us. The Christian lives wholly by the truth of God's Word in Jesus Christ. And it can come only from the outside. In himself he is destitute and dead.

But God has put this Word into the mouth of men in order that it may be communicated to other men. God has willed that we should seek him and find his living Word in the witness of a brother...a Christian needs another Christian who speaks God's Word to him.

The Christ in his own heart is weaker than the Christ in the word of his brother. And that also clarifies the goal of all Christian community: they meet one another as bringers of the message of salvation.

# Mystery

Living without mystery means being ignorant of the mystery of our own life, of the mystery of other people, of the mystery of the world. It means passing over our own hiddenness, the hiddenness of other people and the world. It means being superficial.

It means taking the world seriously only in so far as it can be calculated and exploited, not going behind the world of calculation and utility.

Living without mystery means either failing to see or even denying the decisive matter of life. It means failing to see that the roots of the tree lie in the darkness of the earth, that everything that lives in the light comes from the darkness and hiddenness of a mother's womb, that all our ideas, all our spiritual life comes from the same hidden, mysterious darkness of our body, as all life.

That is something that we do not want to know. We do not want to be told that mystery is the root of all that can be understood and revealed and explained. And if we are told this, we want to quantify this mystery, calculate and explain it, dissect it.

And the result is that we kill life and do not discover the mystery.

## Togetherness and solitude

There are Christians who cannot endure being alone, who hope they will gain some help in association with others.

They are generally disappointed. Then they blame the fellowship for what is really their own fault. The Christian community is not a spiritual sanatorium.

The person who comes into the fellowship because he is running away from himself is misusing it for the sake of diversion. He is really not seeking community at all, but only distraction which will allow him to forget his loneliness.

Let him who cannot be alone beware of community. Alone you stood before God when he called you; alone you had to answer that call; alone you had to struggle and pray.

But the reverse is also true: Let him who is not in community beware of being alone. Into the community you were called; in the community of the called you bear your cross, you struggle, you pray.

If you scorn the fellowship of the brethren, you reject the call of Jesus Christ, and thus your solitude can only be hurtful to you.

Only in the fellowship do we learn to be rightly alone and only in aloneness do we learn to live rightly in the fellowship.

# *Contempt for humanity*

There is a very real danger of our drifting into an attitude of contempt for humanity. We know quite well that we have no right to do so, and that it would lead us into the most sterile relation with our fellow-men.

The following thoughts may keep us from such a temptation. It means that we at once fall into the worst blunders of our opponents. The man who despises another will never be able to understand him.

Nothing that we despise in the other man is entirely absent from ourselves. We often expect from others more than we are willing to do ourselves.

Why have we hitherto thought so intemperately about man and his frailty and temptability? We must learn to regard people less in the light of what they do or omit to do, and more in the light of what they suffer.

The only profitable relationship to others — and especially to our weaker brethren — is one of love, and that means the will to hold fellowship with them. God himself did not despise humanity, but became man for men's sake.

## *God's pilgrim and alien*

I am a sojourner on earth. By that I recognize that I cannot abide here, that my time is short. Nor do I have rights here to possessions or a home. I must receive with gratitude all the good that befalls me, but I must suffer injustice and violence without anyone interceding for me.

I have no firm footing either among people or among things. As a guest I am subject to the laws of the place where I am staying. The earth which feeds me has a right to my labor and my strength.

But because I am nothing but a sojourner on earth, with no rights, no support and no security; because God himself has made me so weak and insignificant, he has given me one firm pledge of my goal: his Word. He will not take this one security from me; he will keep this Word with me, and by it he will allow me to feel my strength.

Where the Word is with me from the beginning, I can find my way in a strange land, my justice in injustice, my support in uncertainty, my strength in work, patience in suffering.

# Baptism

Baptism is not an offer made by man to God, but an offer made by Christ to man. It is grounded solely on the will of Jesus Christ, as expressed in his gracious call.

Baptism is essentially passive—being baptized, suffering the call of Christ. In baptism man becomes Christ's own possession.

When the name of Christ is spoken over the candidate, he becomes a partaker in this Name, and is baptized 'into Jesus Christ.' From that moment he belongs to Jesus Christ. He is wrested from the dominion of the world, and passes into the ownership of Christ.

Baptism therefore betokens a 'breach.' Christ invades the realm of Satan, lays hands on his own, and creates for himself his Church. By this act past and present are rent asunder. The old order is passed away, and all things have become new.

This breach is not effected by man's tearing off his own chains through some unquenchable longing for a new life of freedom. The breach has been effected by Christ long since, and in baptism it is effected in our own lives. The baptized Christian has ceased to belong to the world...he belongs to Christ alone.

# *Passing through*

The life of the Christian community in the world bears permanent witness to the truth that 'the fashion of this world passeth away,' that the time is short, and the Lord is nigh. This thought fills them with joy unspeakable.

The world is growing too small for the Christian community, and all it looks for is the Lord's return. It still walks in the flesh, but with eyes upturned to heaven, whence he for whom they wait will come again.

In the world the Christians are a colony of the true home, they are strangers and aliens in a foreign land, enjoying the hospitality of that land, obeying its laws and honoring its government. They receive with gratitude the requirements of their bodily life, and in all things prove themselves honest, just, chaste, gentle, peaceable, and ready to serve. They are patient and cheerful in suffering, and they glory in tribulation.

But they are only passing through the country. At any moment they may receive the signal to move on. Then they will strike tents, leaving behind them all their worldly friends and connections, and following only the voice of their Lord who calls. They leave the land of their exile, and start their homeward trek to heaven.

## *Cheap grace . . . costly grace*

Cheap grace is the preaching of forgiveness without requiring repentance, baptism without church discipline, communion without confession, absolution without personal confession.

Cheap grace is grace without discipleship, grace without the cross, grace without Jesus Christ, living and incarnate.

Costly grace is the treasure hidden in the field; for the sake of it a man will gladly go and sell all that he has. It is the pearl of great price to buy which the merchant will sell all his goods. It is the kingly rule of Christ, for whose sake a man will pluck out the eye which causes him to stumble. It is the call of Jesus Christ at which the disciple leaves his nets and follows him.

Costly grace is the gospel which must be sought again and again, the gift which must be asked for, the door at which a man must knock.

Such grace is costly because it calls us to follow, and it is grace because it calls us to follow Jesus Christ. It is costly because it costs a man his life, and it is grace because it gives a man the only true life.

# 'Follow me'

On two separate occasions Peter received the call, 'Follow me.' It was the first and last word Jesus spoke to his disciple. A whole life lies between these two calls.

The first occasion was by the lake of Gennesareth, when Peter left his nets and his craft and followed Jesus at his word. The second occasion is when the risen Lord finds him back again at his old trade. Once again it is by the lake of Gennesareth, and once again the call is: 'Follow me.'

Between the two calls lay a whole life of discipleship in the following of Christ. Halfway between them comes Peter's confession, when he acknowledged Jesus as the Christ of God. Three times Peter hears the same proclamation that Christ is his Lord and God — at the beginning, at the end, and at Caesarea Philippi. Each time it is the same grace of Christ which calls to him: 'Follow me.'

Three times on Peter's way did grace arrest him, the one grace proclaimed in three different ways.

In the life of Peter grace and discipleship are inseparable. He had received the grace which costs.

# Justification and sanctification

Justification is the means whereby we appropriate the saving act of God in the past, and sanctification the promise of God's activity in the present and future. Justification secured our entrance into fellowship and communion with Christ through the unique and final event of his death, and sanctification keeps us in that fellowship in Christ.

Justification is primarily concerned with the relation between man and the law of God, sanctification with the Christian's separation from the world until the second coming of Christ.

Justification makes the individual a member of the Church whereas sanctification preserves the Church with all its members.

Justification enables the believer to break away from his sinful past, sanctification enables him to abide in Christ, to persevere in faith and to grow in love.

We may perhaps think of justification and sanctification as bearing the same relation to each other as creation and preservation. Justification is the new creation of the new man, and sanctification his preservation until the day of Jesus Christ.

# *The image of Christ*

God does not neglect his lost creature. He plans to recreate his image in man.

Since fallen man cannot rediscover and assimilate the form of God, the only way is for God to take the form of man and come to him. The Son of God who dwelt in the form of God the Father, lays aside that form, and comes to man in the form of a slave. The change of form, which could not take place in man, now takes place in God.

God sends his Son — here lies the only remedy. It is not enough to give man a new philosophy or a better religion. A Man comes to men.

The image of God has entered our midst...but it is not the same image as Adam bore in the primal glory of paradise. Rather, it is the image of one who enters a world of sin and death, who takes upon himself all the sorrows of humanity, who meekly bears God's wrath and judgment against sinners, and obeys his will with unswerving devotion, the Man born to poverty, the friend of publicans and sinners, the Man of sorrows, rejected of man and forsaken of God.

Here is God made man.

# The harvest field

The Savior looks with compassion on his people, the people of God. He could not rest satisfied with the few who had heard his call and followed. He shrank from the idea of forming an exclusive little coterie with his disciples.

Unlike the founders of the great religions, he had no desire to withdraw them from the vulgar crowd and initiate them into an esoteric system of religion and ethics. He had come, he had worked and suffered for the sake of all his people.

But the disciples wanted to keep him to themselves, as they showed when the young children were brought to him, and on several occasions when he was accosted by beggars on the roadside.

The disciples had to learn that Jesus would not be hemmed in by them in his service. His gospel of the kingdom of God and his power of healing belonged to the sick and poor, wherever they were to be found among his people.

There is now no time to lose: the work of harvest brooks no delay. 'But the laborers are few.' It is hardly surprising that so few are granted to see things with the pitying eyes of Jesus, for only those who share the love of his heart have been given eyes to see.

# *Optimism*

It is wiser to be pessimistic; it is a way of avoiding disappointment and ridicule, and so wise people condemn optimism.

The essence of optimism is not its view of the present, but the fact that it is the inspiration of life and hope when others give in; it enables a man to hold his head high when everything seems to be going wrong; it gives him strength to sustain reverses and yet to claim the future for himself instead of abandoning it to his opponent.

The optimism that is will for the future should never be despised, even if it is proved wrong a hundred times; it is health and vitality.

There are people who regard it as frivolous, and some Christians think it impious for anyone to hope and prepare for a better earthly future.

They think that the meaning of present events is chaos, disorder, and catastrophe; and in resignation or pious escapism they surrender all responsibility for reconstruction and for future generations.

It may be that the day of judgment will dawn tomorrow; in that case, we shall gladly stop working for a better future. But not before.

# The future Church

The Church is the Church only when it exists for others. To make a start, it should give away all its property to those in need. The clergy must live solely on the free-will offerings of their congregations, or possibly engage in some secular calling.

The Church must share in the secular problems of ordinary human life, not dominating, but helping and serving. It must tell men of every calling what it means to live in Christ, to exist for others.

In particular, our own Church will have to take the field against the vices of 'hubris,' power-worship, envy and humbug as the roots of all evil. It will have to speak of moderation, purity, trust, loyalty, constancy, patience, discipline, humility, contentment and modesty.

It must not underestimate the importance of human example (which has its origin in the humanity of Jesus and is so important in Paul's teaching); it is not abstract argument, but example, that gives its word emphasis and power.

## *The view from below*

There remains an experience of incomparable value, namely that we have learned to see the great events of world history from below, from the perspective of those who are excluded, under suspicion, ill-treated, powerless, oppressed and scorned, in short, those who suffer.

That is the case, provided that at this time bitterness and envy have not eaten away at our hearts; that we look on things great and small, on sorrow and joy, on strength and weakness, with new eyes; that our perception of what is great, human, just and merciful has become clearer, freer, more incorruptible, indeed that personal suffering is a more useful key, a more fruitful principle for opening up the world in thought and action than personal happiness.

The important thing is that this perspective from below should not turn into support for those who are eternally discontented, but that we do justice to life in all its dimensions, and thus affirm it, from a higher content which is really beyond 'above' and 'below.'

## *The hound of heaven*

Not to be able to get away from God is the disturbing restriction on any Christian life. Those who accept it, who allow themselves to be persuaded by God, cannot get away, just as a child cannot get away from its mother or a husband from the wife whom he loved.

Anyone to whom God has once spoken can never again completely forget him; God continues to go with him, in good or ill; God follows a man, like his shadow.

And this enduring nearness of God becomes too much for a man, too big; it is stronger than he, and he may well think, 'If only I had never encountered God! It is too hard for me, it destroys my peace of mind and my happiness.'

No longer to be able to get away from God means much anxiety, much despondency, much tribulation, but it also means never being able to be Godless, in good times and in bad. It means God with us on all our ways, in faith and in sin, in persecution, mockery and death.

He holds us fast. He will not let us go. Lord, always persuade us anew and overpower us.

# *His acceptance of guilt*

Jesus is not concerned with the proclamation and realization of new ethical ideas; he is not concerned with himself being good; he is concerned solely with love for the real man, and for that reason he is able to enter into the fellowship of the guilt of men and to take the burden of their guilt upon himself.

Jesus does not desire to be regarded as the only perfect one at the expense of men; he does not desire to look down on mankind as the only guiltless one while mankind goes to its ruin under the weight of its guilt; he does not wish that some idea of a new man should triumph amid the wreckage of a humanity whose guilt has destroyed it.

He does not wish to acquit himself of the guilt under which men die. A love which left man alone in his guilt would not be love for the real man.

As one who acts responsibly in the historical existence of men Jesus becomes guilty.

It must be emphasized that it is solely his love which makes him incur guilt. From his selfless love, from his freedom from sin, Jesus enters into the guilt of men and takes this guilt upon himself.

# Christ's large-heartedness

Christ kept himself from suffering till his hour had come, but when it did come he met it as a free man, seized it, and mastered it.

Christ, so the Scriptures tell us, bore the sufferings of all humanity in his own body as if they were his own — a thought beyond our comprehension — accepting them of his own free will.

We are certainly not Christ; we are not called on to redeem the world by our own deeds and sufferings, and we need not try to assume such an impossible burden. We are not lords, but instruments in the hand of the Lord of history; and we can share in other peoples' sufferings only to a very limited degree.

We are not Christ, but if we want to be Christians, we must have some share in Christ's large-heartedness by acting with responsibilty and in freedom when the hour of danger comes, and by showing a real sympathy that springs, not from fear, but from the liberating and redeeming love of Christ for all who suffer.

Mere waiting and looking-on is not Christian behavior. The Christian is called to sympathy and action.

## Love of the enemy

The Christian must treat his enemy as a brother, and requite his hostility with love. His behavior must be determined not by the way others treat him, but by the treatment he himself receives from Jesus.

By our enemies Jesus means those who are quite intractable and utterly unresponsive to our love, who forgive us nothing when we forgive them all, who requite our love with hatred and our service with derision.

No sacrifice which a lover would make for his beloved is too great for us to make for our enemy.

If out of love for our brother we are willing to sacrifice goods, honor, and life, we must be prepared to do the same for our enemy.

Through the medium of prayer we go to our enemy, stand by his side, and plead for him to God. Jesus does not promise that when we bless our enemies and do good to them they will not despitefully use and persecute us. They certainly will.

But not even that can hurt or overcome us so long as we pray for them. For if we pray for them, we are taking their distress and poverty, their guilt and perdition upon ourselves, and pleading to God for them.

**84**

## The gateway to our home

Who knows how near he may already be to the end? Both young and old should reflect that life only begins when it ends here, that all this is only an overture before closed curtains.

So why are we so anxious in thinking about death? Why are we so sad when we imagine ourselves lying on our deathbed? Death is only fearful for the one who is anxious, who fears it.

Death is not wild and terrible, provided that we are still and hold to God's Word. Death is not bitter if we are not embittered. Death is grace, God's greatest grace, which he sends to those who believe in him.

Death is gentle, death is sweet, death is soft, death calls us with heavenly power provided that we know that it is the gateway to our home, to the tent of joy, to the eternal realm of peace.

Perhaps we might say: I'm not afraid of death but I am afraid of dying. Who knows that dying is something terrible? Who knows whether the anxiety and distress of men and women is not just trembling and shuddering before the most glorious. most heavenly, most blessed event in the world?

# The joy of God

Joy belongs, not only to those who have been called home, but also to the living, and no one shall take it from us. We are one with them in this joy, but never in sorrow.

How shall we be able to help those who have become joyless and fearful unless we ourselves are supported by courage and joy?

I don't mean by this something fabricated, compelled, but something given, free. Joy dwells with God; it descends from him and seizes spirit, soul, and body, and where this joy has grasped a man it grows greater, carries him away, opens closed doors.

There is a joy which knows nothing of sorrow, need and anxiety of the heart; it has no duration, and it can only drug one for the moment.

The joy of God has been through the poverty of the crib and the distress of the cross; therefore it is insuperable, irrefutable. It does not deny the distress where it is, but finds God in the midst of it, indeed precisely there; it does not contest the most grievous sin, but finds forgiveness in just this way; it looks death in the face, yet finds life in death itself.

# The pure heart

'Blessed are the pure in heart: for they shall see God.' Who is pure in heart? Only those who have surrendered their hearts completely to Jesus. Only those whose hearts are undefiled by their own evil — and by their own virtues too.

The pure in heart have a childlike simplicity like Adam before the fall, innocent alike of good and evil.

If men renounce their own good, if in penitence they have renounced their own hearts, if they rely solely upon Jesus, then his word purifies their hearts.

Purity of heart is here contrasted with all outward purity, even the purity of high intentions. The pure heart is pure alike of good and evil, it belongs exclusively to Christ and looks only to him who goes on before.

Only they will see God, who in this life have looked solely unto Jesus Christ, the Son of God. For them their hearts are free from all defiling phantasies and are not distracted by conflicting desires and intentions.

They are wholly absorbed by the contemplation of God. They shall see God, whose hearts have become a reflection of the image of Jesus Christ.

## An end of death

Does it not seem to us again and again in the early deaths of Christians as though God were robbing himself of his best instruments at a time when he needed them most? But God makes no mistakes.

Does God perhaps need our brothers for some hidden service for us in the heavenly world? We should restrain our human thoughts, which always seek to know more than they can, and keep to what is certain.

We know that God and the Devil are locked together in combat over the world and that the Devil has a word to say even at death. In the face of death we cannot say, in a fatalistic way, 'It is God's will'; we must add the opposite: 'It is not God's will.'

Death shows that the world is not what it should be, but that it needs redemption. Christ alone overcomes death. God's will is the overcoming of death through the death of Jesus Christ.

Only in the cross and resurrection of Jesus Christ has death come under God's power. Only in the cross and resurrection of Jesus Christ must it serve the purpose of God. Not a fatalistic surrender, but living faith in Jesus Christ can seriously make an end of death for us.

## No distinction

God loves man. God loves the world. It is not an ideal man that he loves, but man as he is; not an ideal world, but the real world.

What we find abominable in man's opposition to God, what we shrink back from with pain and hostility, the real man, the real world, this is for God the ground for unfathomable love, and it is with this that he unites himself utterly.

God becomes man, real man. While we are trying to grow out beyond our manhood, to leave the man behind us, God becomes man and we have to recognize that God wishes us men, too, to be real men.

While we are distinguishing the pious from the ungodly, the good from the wicked, the noble from the mean, God makes no distinction at all in his love for the real man. He does not permit us to classify men and the world according to our own standards and to set ourselves up as judges over them. He leads us by himself becoming a real man and a companion of sinners and thereby compelling us to become the judges of God.

God sides with the real man and with the real world against all their accusers.

## To suffer with men

Some of us suffer a great deal from having our senses dulled in the face of all the sorrows which these war years have brought with them. And yet we must be careful not to confuse ourselves with Christ.

Christ endured all suffering and all human guilt to the full. But Christ could suffer alongside men because at the same time he was able to redeem them from suffering.

We are not called to burden ourselves with the sorrows of the whole world; in the end, we cannot suffer with men in our own strength because we are unable to redeem. A suppressed desire to suffer with man in one's own strength must become resignation. We are simply called to look with utter joy on the one who really suffered with men and became their Redeemer.

We may joyfully believe that there was, there is, a man to whom no human sorrow and no human sin is strange and who in the profoundest love achieved our redemption.

Only in such joy towards Christ, the Redeemer, are we saved from having our senses dulled by the pressure of human sorrow, or from becoming resigned under the experience of suffering.

# The firm ground

The key to everything is the 'in him'. All that we may rightly expect from God, and ask him for, is to be found in Jesus Christ.

The God of Jesus Christ has nothing to do with what God, as we imagine him, could do and ought to do. If we are to learn what God promises, and what he fulfills, we must persevere in quiet meditation on the life, sayings, deeds, sufferings and death of Jesus.

It is certain that we may always live close to God and in the light of his presence, and that such living is an entirely new life for us; that nothing is then impossible for us, because all things are possible with God; that no earthly power can touch us without his will, and that danger and distress can only drive us closer to him.

It is certain that we can claim nothing for ourselves, and may yet pray for everything; it is certain that our joy is hidden in suffering, and our life in death; it is certain that in all this we are in a fellowship that sustains us.

In Jesus God has said Yes and Amen to it all, and that Yes and Amen is the firm ground on which we stand.

# Powers of good

I am so sure of God's guiding hand that I hope I shall always be kept in that certainty. You must never doubt that I'm travelling with gratitude and cheerfulness along the road where I'm being led. My past life is brim-full of God's goodness, and my sins are covered by the forgiving love of Christ crucified. I'm most thankful for the people I have met, and I only hope that they never have to grieve about me, but that they, too, will always be certain of, and thankful for, God's mercy and forgiveness.

With every power for good to stay and guide me,
comforted and inspired beyond all fear,
I'll live these days with you in thought beside me,
and pass, with you, into the coming year.
The old year still torments our hearts, unhastening;
the long days of our sorrow still endure;
Father, grant to the soul thou hast been chastening
that thou hast promised, the healing and the cure.
Should it be ours to drain the cup of grieving
even to the dregs of pain, at thy command,
we will not falter, thankfully receiving
all that is given by thy loving hand.

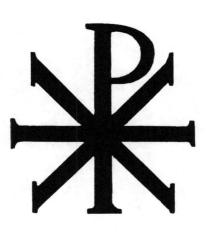

# Sources and index

In the index, the figures in bold type refer to the pages of Readings in this book. They are followed by the Sources (see list of abbreviations).

*COD The Cost of Discipleship*, Macmillan
CP Collected Papers (*Gesammelte Schriften II*), Harper/Collins
*E Ethics,* Macmillan
*LPP Letters and Papers from Prison,* Macmillan
*LT Life Together,* Harper/Collins
S Sermons (*Predigten* I and II), Christian Kaiser
*TP True Patriotism,* Harper/Collins

**25** *LT* p. 17
**26** *LT* pp. 59,60
**27** *LT* pp. 70, 71
**28** *LT* pp. 75, 76
**29** *LT* 77, 78
**30** *LT* pp. 81, 82
**31** *LT* p. 86
**32** *LT* pp. 89, 90
**33** *COD* p. 49
**34** *COD* pp. 52, 53
**35** *COD* pp. 77, 78
**36** *COD* p. 82
**39** *COD* pp. 84-90
**40** *COD* p. 102
**41** *COD* pp. 112-14
**42** *COD* pp. 127-30
**43** *COD* pp. 141-4

**44** *COD* pp. 145-7
**45** *COD* pp.148-50
**46** *COD* pp. 155-6
**47** *COD* p. 170
**48** *LPP* pp. 44, 46
**49** *LPP* pp. 191, 192
**50** *LPP* p. 203
**53** *LPP* pp. 217, 218
**54** *LPP* p. 232
**55** *LPP* pp. 278-81
**56** *LPP* pp. 281, 282
**57** *LPP* p. 300
**58** *LPP* pp. 311, 312
**59** *LPP* pp. 360, 361
**60** *LPP* pp. 361, 362
**61** S II pp. 185-9
**62** *LT* pp. 7-17

**63** S I p. 446  **78** CP p. 441
**63** *LT* p. 57  **81** S I p. 430
**67** *LT* p. 2  **82** *E* p. 209
**68** S II p. 431  **83** *LPP* p. 14
**69** *COD* pp. 206, 207  **84** *LPP*
**70** *COD* pp. 243, 244  **85** S I p. 400
**71** *COD* pp. 36, 37  **86** *TP* p. 189
**72** *COD* pp. 37, 38  **87** *COD* p. 101
**73** *COD* p. 250  **88** *TP* pp. 124ff.
**74** *COD* pp. 270, 271  **89** *E* pp. 52-6
**75** *COD* pp. 179, 180, 181  **90** *TP* p. 189
**76** *LPP* p. 15  **91** *LPP* p. 391
**77** *LPP* pp. 282, 283  **92** *LPP* pp. 393-400

The extracts from the following are reprinted by permission of Macmillan Publishing Co., *The Cost of Discipleship* (trans. R. H. Fuller, English translation © SCM Press Ltd, 1959); *Ethics* (trans. Neville Horton Smith, English translation copyright © SCM Press Ltd 1955); *Letters and Papers from Prison* (trans. R. H. Fuller, Frank Clark and John Bowden, English translation copyright © SCM Press Ltd 1953, 1967, 1971); hitherto untranslated material from *Gesammelte Schriften II* (Christian Kaiser 1978) and *Predigten* I and II (Christian Kaiser 1984, 1985) trans. © John Bowden 1986. The extract from *True Patriotism* is reprinted by permission of Christian Kaiser Verlag and those from *Life Together* © 1954 Harper and Row Inc. by permission of Harper/Collins Publishers.